LITTLE C  R

BOLD AND EASY COLORING BOOK

54 coloring pages, featuring Bold and Easy Designs for Adults, Teens and Kids.

PUBLISHED IN 2025 BY PAGE PUBLICATIONS

LITTLE CORNER
BOLD AND EASY COLORING BOOK

Place a piece of paper behind your artwork to prevent bleed through.

this book belongs to

_____

_____

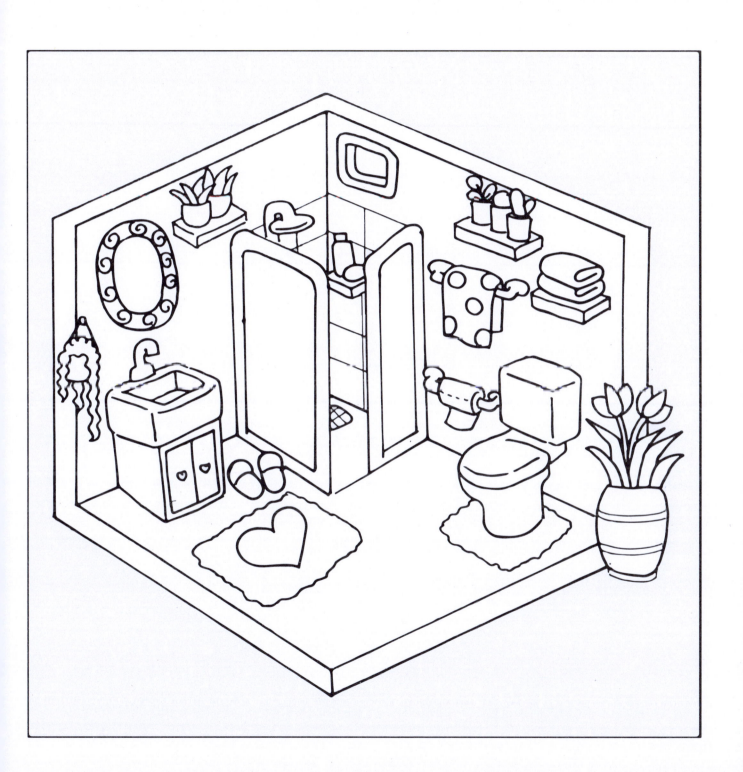

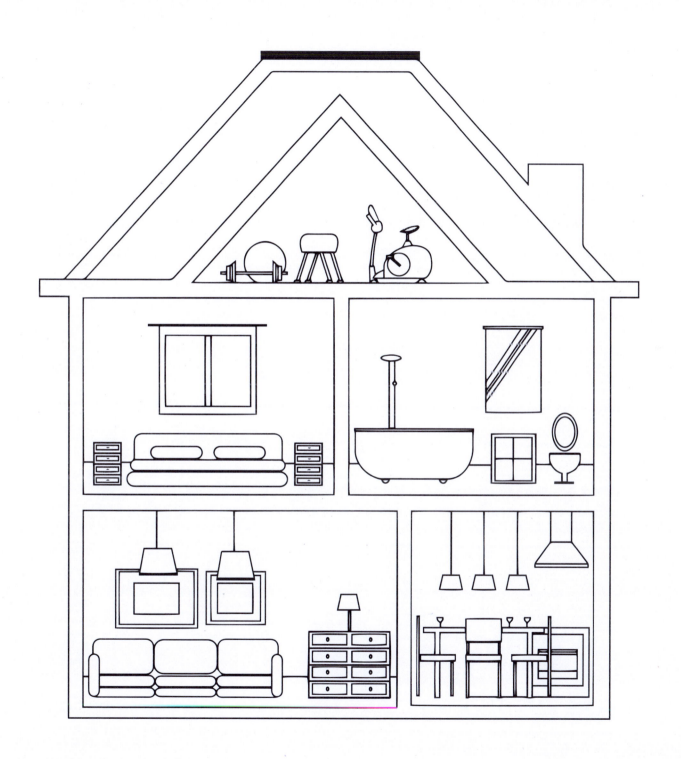

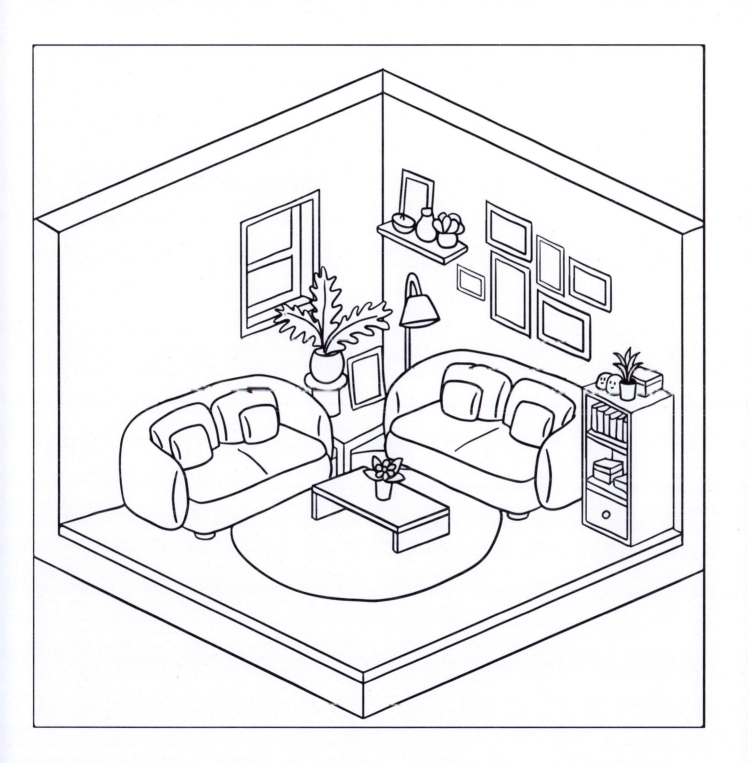

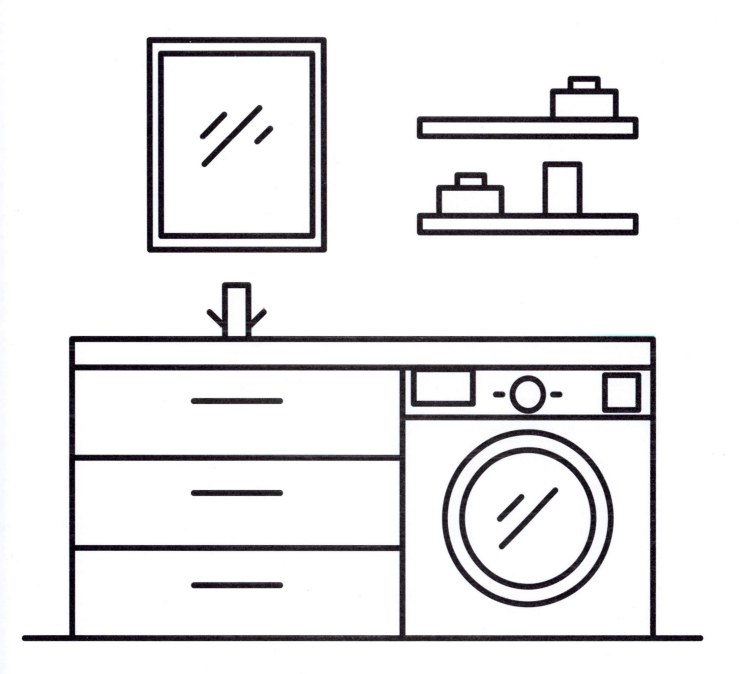

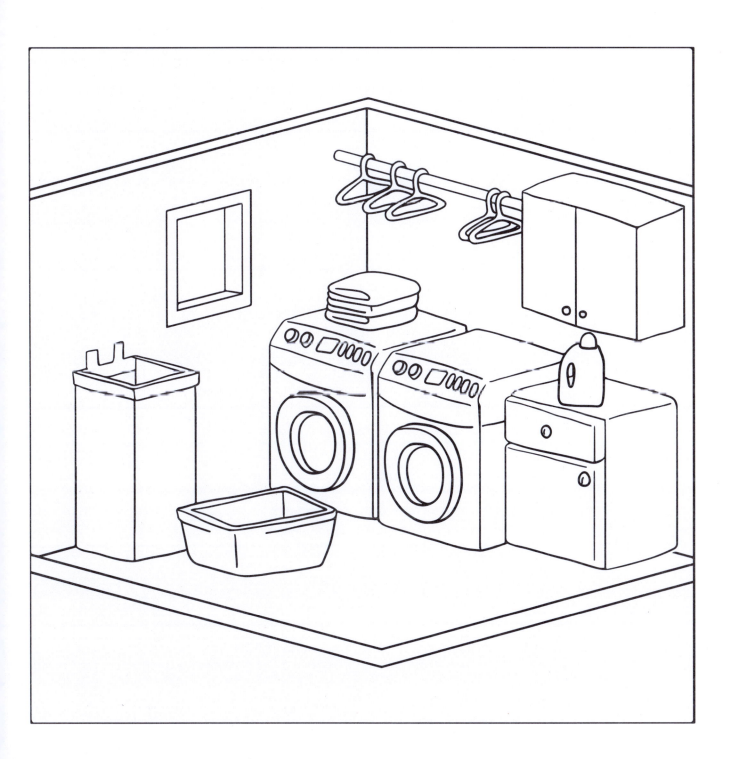